Do not fear, for I am with you;
do not be afraid, for I am your God.
I will strengthen you; I will help you;
I will hold on to you with my righteous right hand.
~Isaiah 41:10~

> *Be strong and courageous;
> don't be terrified or afraid of
> them. For the LORD your God
> is the one who will go with
> you; he will not leave your or
> abandon you.*
> *~Deuteronomy 31:6~*

Therefore we do not give up. Even though our outer person is being destroyed, our inner person is being renewed day by day.
~2 Corinthians 4:16–18~

*Trust in the LORD with all
your heart, and do not rely on
your own understanding.
~Proverbs 3:5~*

Because of the LORD's faithful love we do not perish, for his mercies never end. They are new every morning; great is your faithfulness!
~Lamentations 3:22–23~

*Do nothing out of selfish
ambition or conceit,
but in humility consider
others as more important
than yourselves.
~Philippians 2:3~*

Let us run with endurance the race that lies before us, keeping our eyes on Jesus, the source and perfecter of our faith.
~Hebrews 12:1–2~

> *The one who walks with the wise will become wise, but a companion of fools will suffer harm.*
> ~Proverbs 13:20~

> "The LORD your God is among you, a warrior who saves. He will rejoice over you with gladness. He will be quiet in his love. He will delight in you with singing.
> ~Zephaniah 3:17~

Trust in the LORD forever,
because in the LORD, the LORD
himself, is an everlasting rock!
~Isaiah 26:4~

The Lord does not delay his promise, as some understand delay, but is patient with you, not wanting any to perish but all to come to repentance.
~2 Peter 3:9~

> *Blessed is the one who endures trials, because when he has stood the test he will receive the crown of life that God has promised to those who love him.*
> *~James 1:12~*

Do not be conformed to this age, but be transformed by the renewing of your mind, so that you may discern what is the good, pleasing, and perfect will of God.
~Romans 12:2~